· FUN · WITH · MATHS ·

SHAPES AND SOLIDS

LAKSHMI HEWAVISENTI

Gloucester Press
London · New York · Toronto · Sydney

© Aladdin Books Ltd 1991

All rights reserved

Created and designed by
N.W. Books
28 Percy Street
London W1P 9FF

Design: David West
Children's Book Design
Editor: Melanie Halton
Illustrators: John Kelly
Ian Moores

First published in Great Britain
in 1991 by
Franklin Watts Ltd
96 Leonard Street
London
EC2A 4RH

ISBN 0-7496-0557-X

Printed in Belgium

A CIP catalogue record for this
book is available from the British
Library.

CONTENTS

INTRODUCTION

Do you know the difference between shapes and solids? We are surrounded by them in everyday life. You can have great fun with the exciting activities in this book. Each one will help you learn more about many different shapes and solids around you.

MIRROR IMAGES

Mirrors can be fun to use and can help us see the other side of half-drawn objects. Sometimes the other side isn't as obvious as it seems!

What to do
Draw a line on some paper. On one side of the line draw half a picture (like half a face). You could ask a friend to guess and draw the other side. Use a mirror to see if your friend was right.

What you need

Paper

Mirror

Pencil

Coloured pencils

How to use the mirror
To check with a mirror, put it on the line you drew. Can you see the whole picture ?

Here are some more ideas
for you to try – a beetle and
a cross shape.

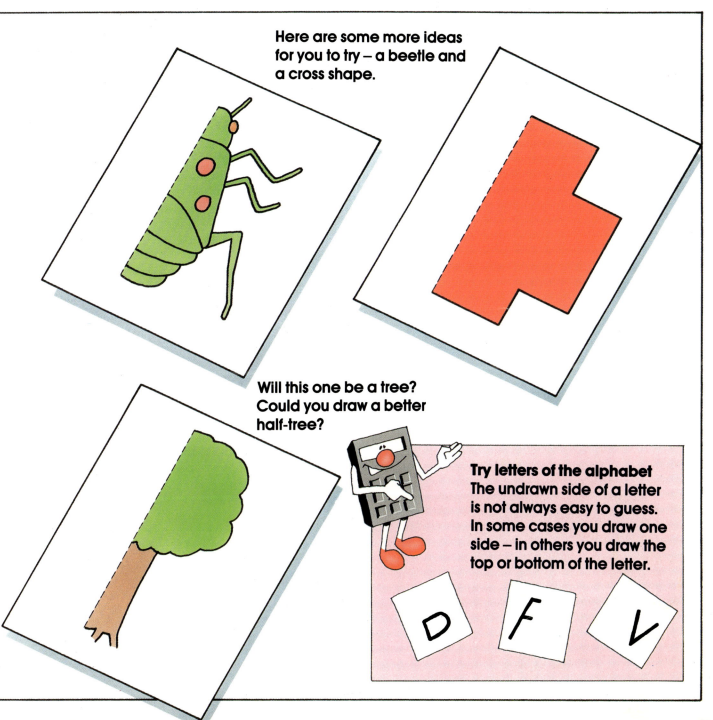

Will this one be a tree?
Could you draw a better
half-tree?

Try letters of the alphabet
The undrawn side of a letter
is not always easy to guess.
In some cases you draw one
side – in others you draw the
top or bottom of the letter.

D F V

CIRCLES

Circles are all around us. You can use them to make interesting pictures.

What to do
Draw a circle with a compass. Now, *without adjusting the compass*, put the point anywhere on the edge and draw half a circle. Move the point to where the half circle ends, and draw another half circle. Keep moving the point and drawing half circles to make a flower.

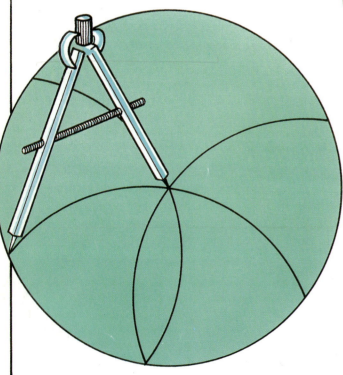

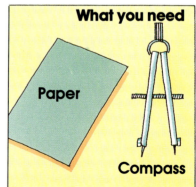

What you need

Paper

Compass

Drawing characters with circles
The teddy bear below has been drawn using circles. Try using your compass (or different round objects) to draw similar pictures.

Caterpillar

Teddy bear

A caterpillar can be drawn using a compass or coin. Draw circles which overlap. Now go over the outline only. You can then rub out bits you don't need.

BICYCLE WHEEL

When using round shapes we sometimes need to know their "length", or the distance around them. This is known as the circumference. Here is one way of working out round length.

What to do
Use chalk to mark the point where the bicycle wheel touches the ground. Mark the ground as well. Call it "A". Ask your friend to ride slowly until the wheel mark is on the ground again. Mark the ground again and call this new point "B".

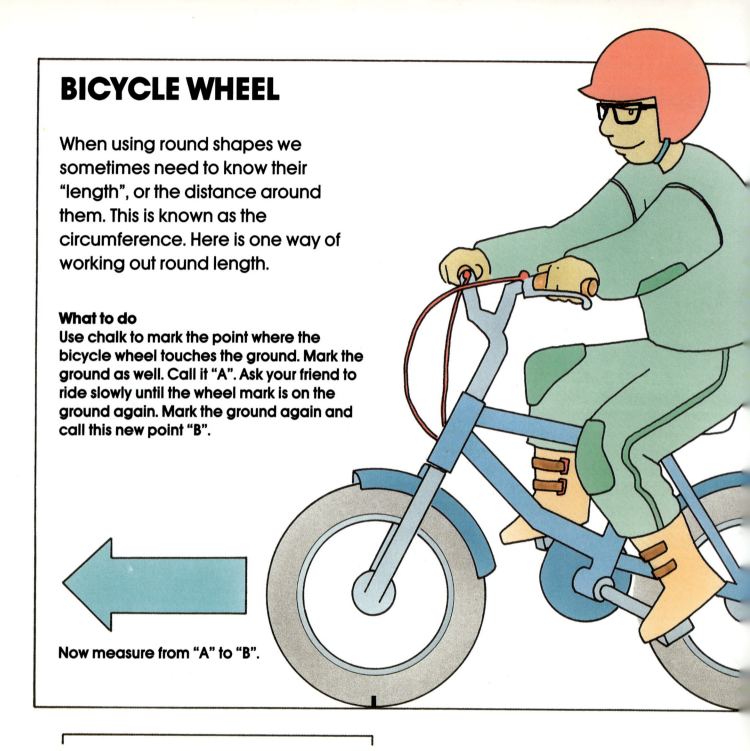

Now measure from "A" to "B".

B   A

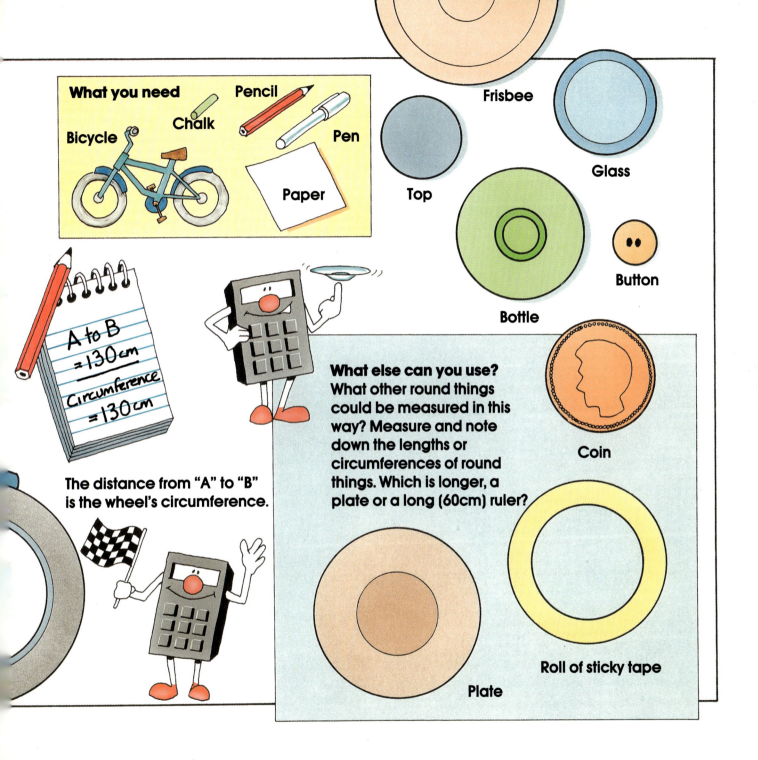

What you need

Pencil

Chalk

Bicycle

Pen

Paper

Frisbee

Glass

Top

Button

Bottle

A to B
=130cm

Circumference
=130cm

What else can you use?
What other round things
could be measured in this
way? Measure and note
down the lengths or
circumferences of round
things. Which is longer, a
plate or a long (60cm) ruler?

Coin

The distance from "A" to "B"
is the wheel's circumference.

Plate

Roll of sticky tape

9

CURVED LINES

Believe it or not, sometimes straight lines can appear to be curves! The trick is to draw the lines in a special way. As the lines cross, your eyes see them "bending"!

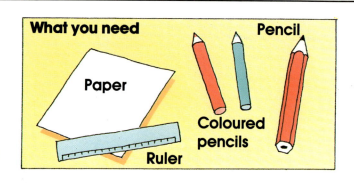

What you need

Paper

Pencil

Coloured pencils

Ruler

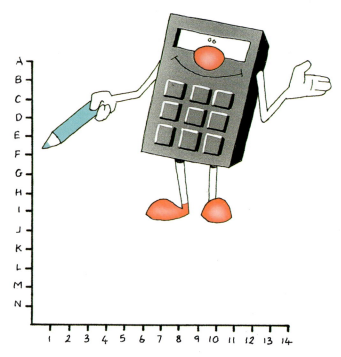

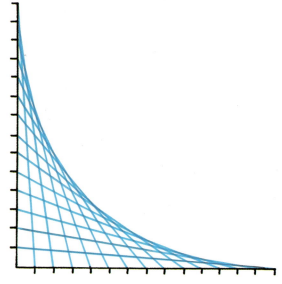

What to do
Using a ruler, draw a grid like the one above. Make fourteen regularly spaced marks on the edges. Leave enough room to fit in the number and letter labels.

Now, using your ruler and a coloured pencil, connect A to 1, B to 2, C to 3 and so on. The curve will start to appear after you've drawn four or five lines.

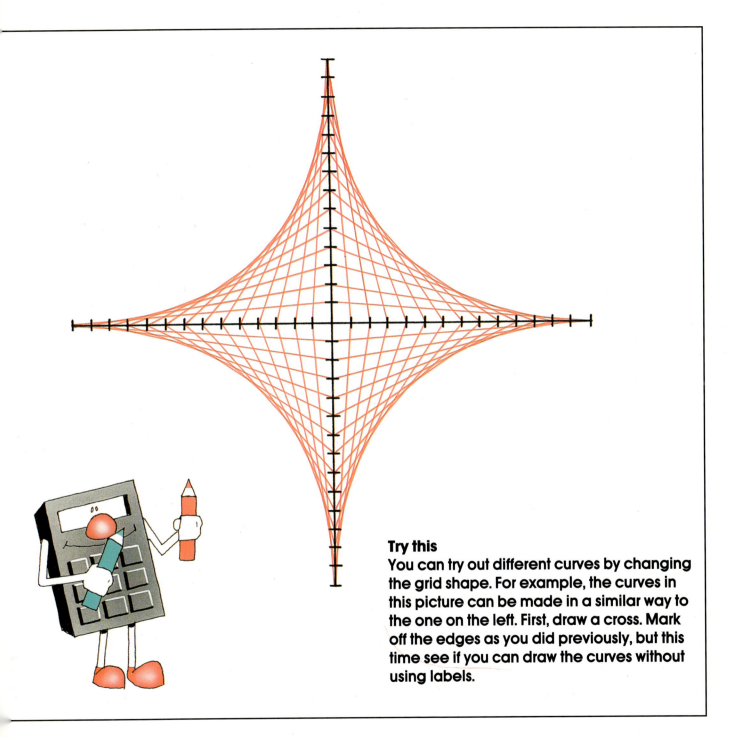

Try this
You can try out different curves by changing the grid shape. For example, the curves in this picture can be made in a similar way to the one on the left. First, draw a cross. Mark off the edges as you did previously, but this time see if you can draw the curves without using labels.

PLAYING WITH SHAPES

There are lots of shapes around us, and many have special names, like squares, rectangles or triangles. Each different shape has certain aspects that help us tell them apart.

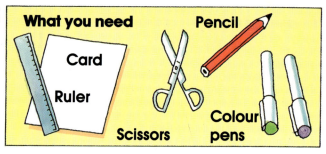

What you need

Card
Ruler
Pencil
Scissors
Colour pens

To trace this, see opposite page.

What to do
Trace this shape on to card. Go over the lines using a ruler so that all the shapes can be seen clearly. The shapes can now be coloured and cut out. You should have ten pieces in all.

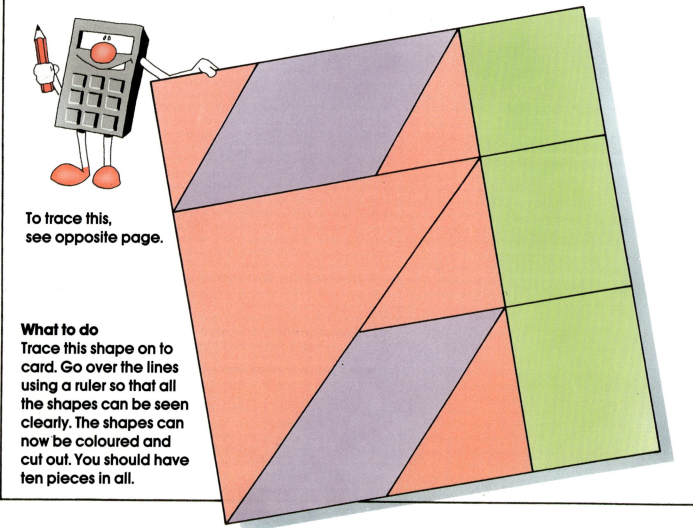

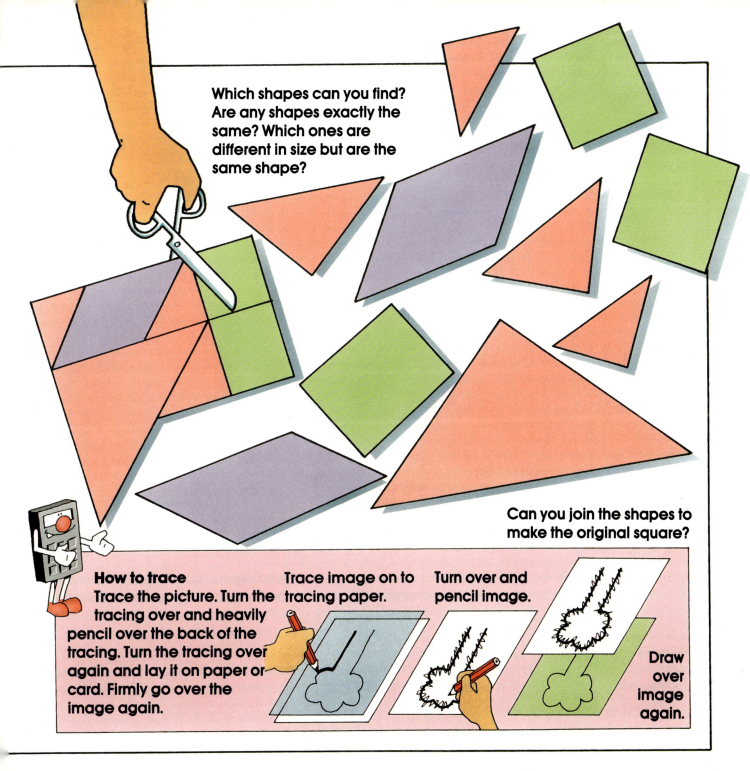

Which shapes can you find? Are any shapes exactly the same? Which ones are different in size but are the same shape?

Can you join the shapes to make the original square?

How to trace
Trace the picture. Turn the tracing over and heavily pencil over the back of the tracing. Turn the tracing over again and lay it on paper or card. Firmly go over the image again.

Trace image on to tracing paper.

Turn over and pencil image.

Draw over image again.

TANGRAMS

A tangram is a square which is cut up into seven pieces so that the pieces can be used to make interesting pictures. They can be put together in lots of ways.

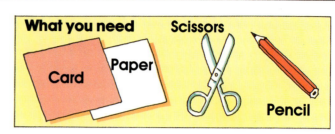

What you need

Card Paper Scissors Pencil

To trace this, see pg. 13.

What to do
To make tangram pictures, first trace this big square (and the lines) on to card. Go over the lines with a ruler, and then colour and cut out the seven pieces. Now you are ready to play around with the pieces!

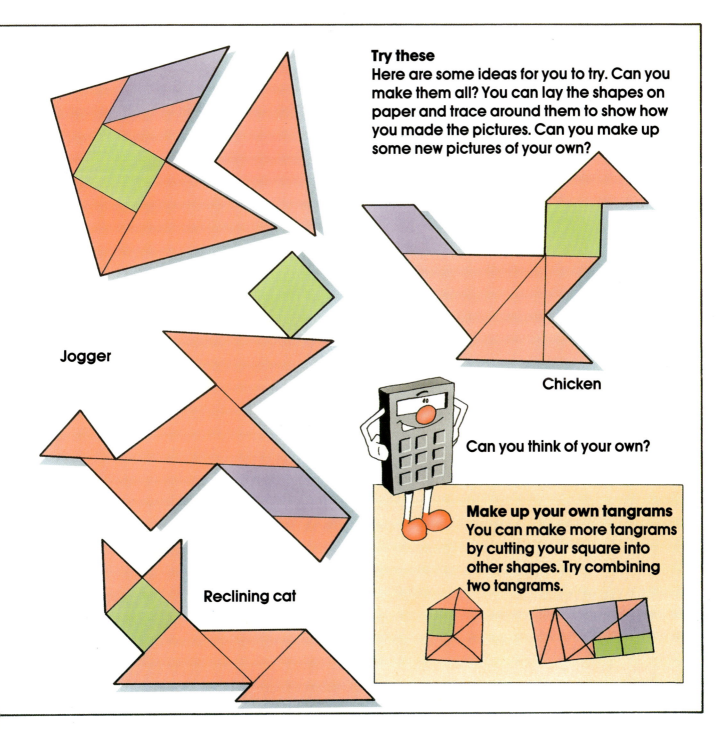

Try these
Here are some ideas for you to try. Can you make them all? You can lay the shapes on paper and trace around them to show how you made the pictures. Can you make up some new pictures of your own?

Jogger

Chicken

Can you think of your own?

Reclining cat

Make up your own tangrams
You can make more tangrams by cutting your square into other shapes. Try combining two tangrams.

SHAPE SIZES

This activity is about looking at the area (space inside) of shapes. Sometimes it is obvious when one shape is bigger than another – at other times a grid could help.

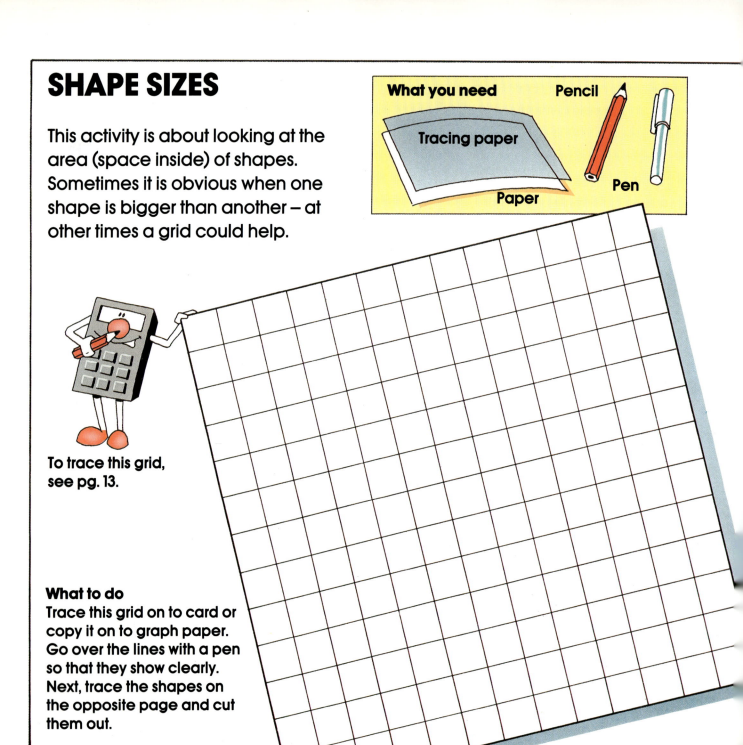

What you need

Pencil

Tracing paper

Paper

Pen

To trace this grid, see pg. 13.

What to do
Trace this grid on to card or copy it on to graph paper. Go over the lines with a pen so that they show clearly. Next, trace the shapes on the opposite page and cut them out.

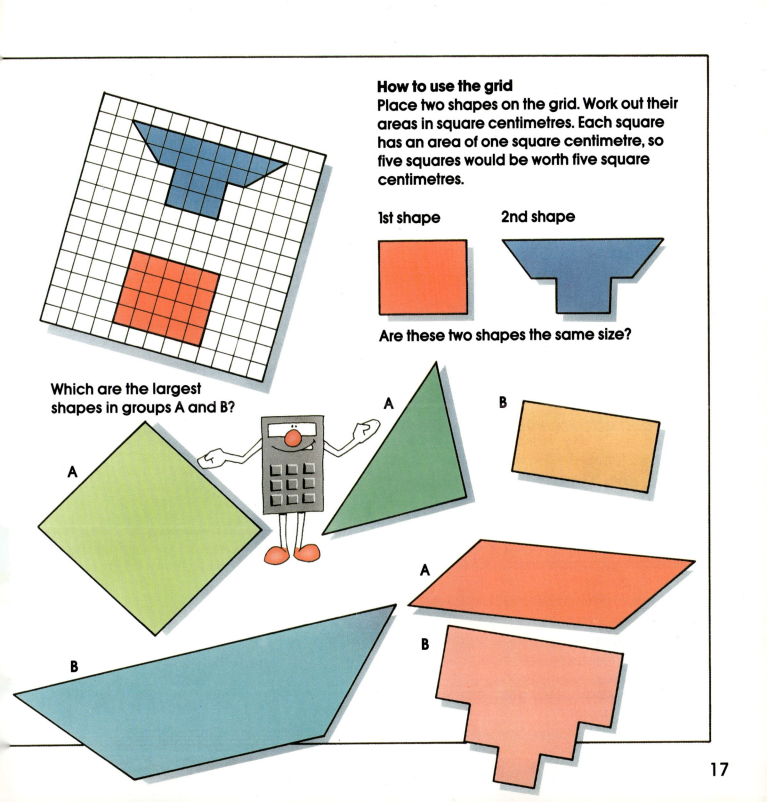

How to use the grid

Place two shapes on the grid. Work out their areas in square centimetres. Each square has an area of one square centimetre, so five squares would be worth five square centimetres.

1st shape

2nd shape

Are these two shapes the same size?

Which are the largest shapes in groups A and B?

A

B

A

A

B

B

17

TESSELLATION

Tessellating patterns are made up of lots of small patterns with the same design. You can make all sorts of exciting patterns. First of all you will have to draw your designs.

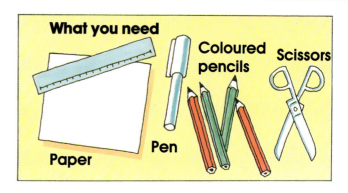

What you need

Paper

Pen

Coloured pencils

Scissors

What to do
Cut lots of squares of the same size. On each one draw the same pattern – here is an idea you may like to try.

To make your squares match exactly, it will help to use a ruler. Mark the edges to show where each part of your pattern should be. Then connect your lines.

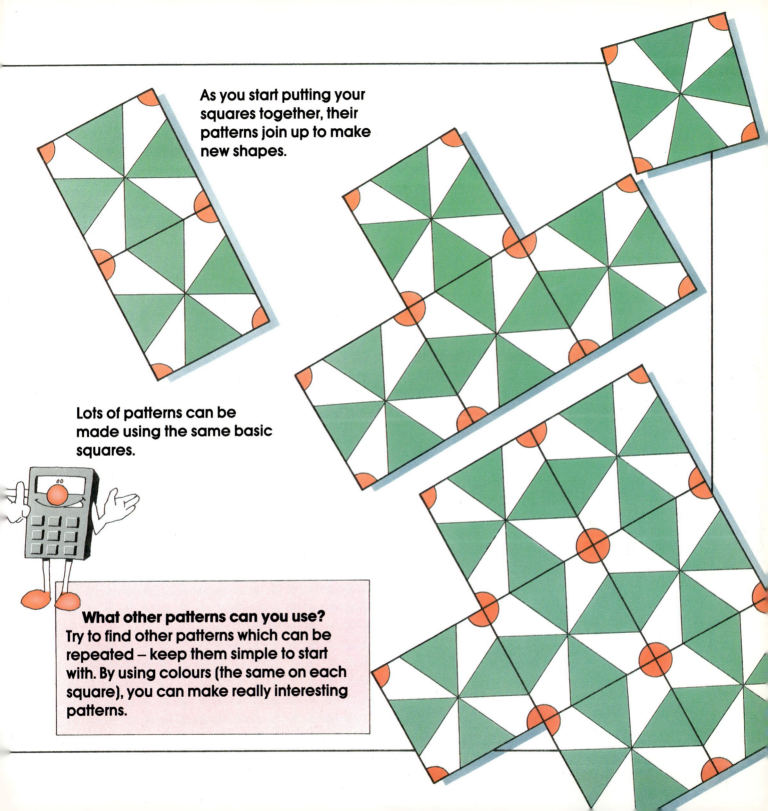

As you start putting your squares together, their patterns join up to make new shapes.

Lots of patterns can be made using the same basic squares.

What other patterns can you use? Try to find other patterns which can be repeated – keep them simple to start with. By using colours (the same on each square), you can make really interesting patterns.

POTATO PRINTS

You will be amazed at what you can make using a potato! They are easy to cut into the shape you want, so you can make your own "stamps". Check with an adult that you are using a safe knife.

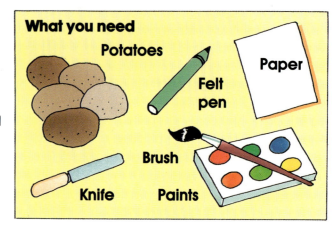

What you need

Potatoes
Felt pen
Paper
Brush
Knife
Paints

How to make it
Start by cutting a potato in half. Use a felt pen to draw your shape. Cut off the bits around the shape so that it stands out a bit.

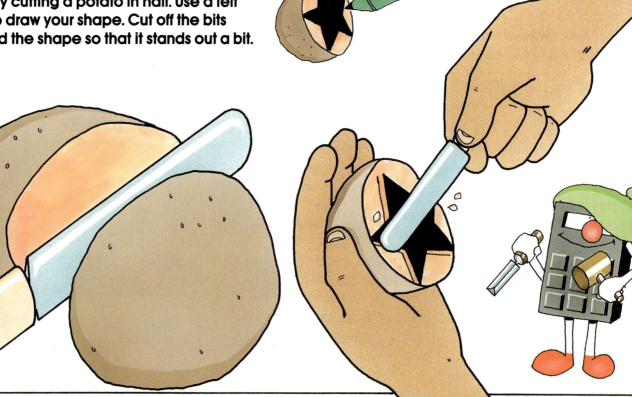

How to print

Paint carefully over the shape. Stamp it firmly on paper, and your print should show when you lift the potato. If you want it darker, just use more paint.

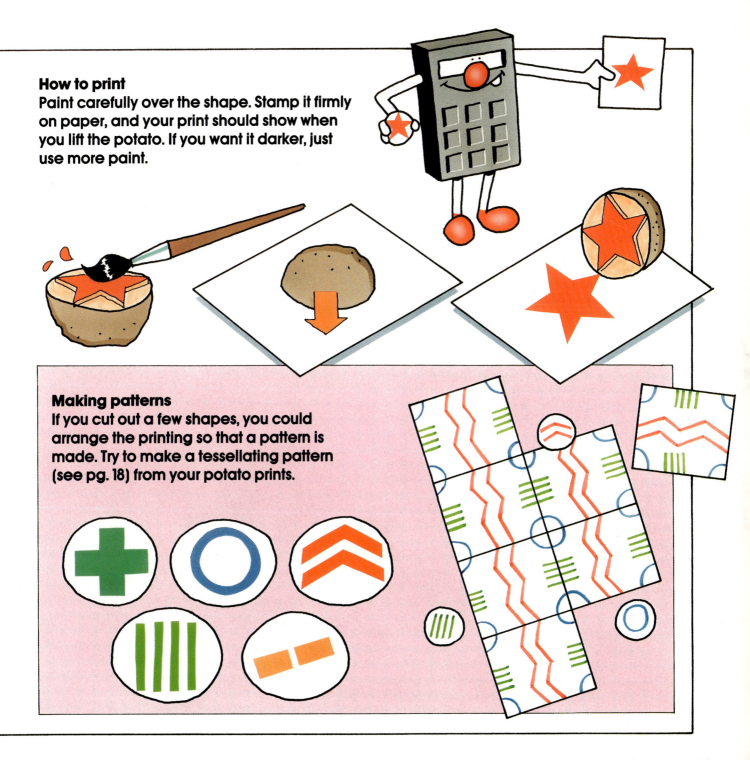

Making patterns

If you cut out a few shapes, you could arrange the printing so that a pattern is made. Try to make a tessellating pattern (see pg. 18) from your potato prints.

COMPASS SHAPES

A compass, paper and colours are all you need to make some great designs. Here are a few ideas for you to start off with.

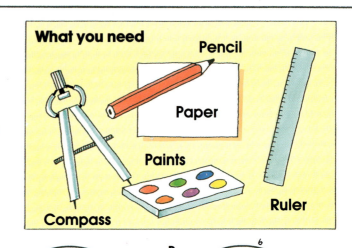

What you need

Pencil

Paper

Paints

Ruler

Compass

Try this design
Draw a circle with a compass (A). Divide your circle into eight parts, using a ruler (B). Put the compass point on the edge of the circle where you have marked and draw a curve within the circle (C). Do this eight times.

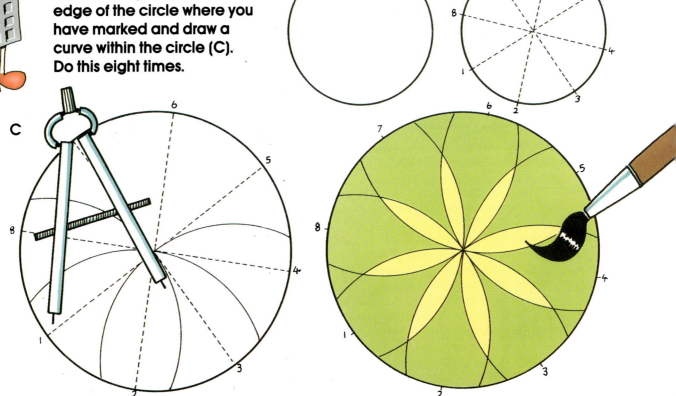

Try this
Draw a circle with a compass. Next, put your compass point on the edge of the circle and draw another. Now, put your compass point on a place where the first two circles cross, and draw another. Continue all the way round your original circle.

Use colours for effect.

Can you draw this?
Here's a difficult one for you to try – the trick is to use more than one size of circle. Try lots more of your own and display them!

ONE-SIDED SHAPE

This activity, also known as the Möbius Strip, will really test your skill. By using a simple piece of paper you can have a lot of fun making paper shapes.

What to do
Find a very long strip of paper. Twist it once and glue or tape the ends together (1). Next, draw a line down the middle (2). You now have a one-sided shape.

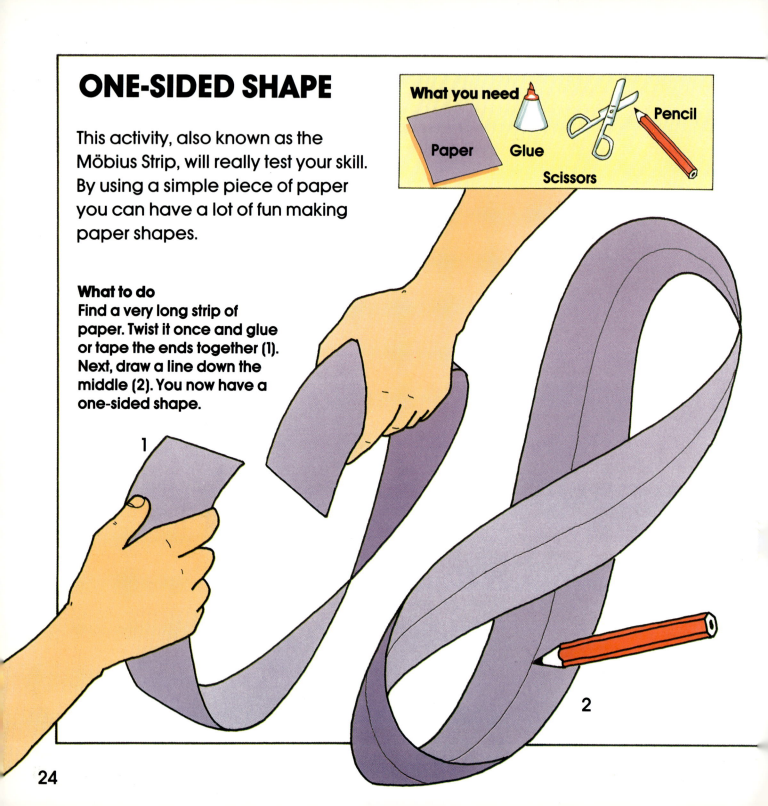

What you need

Paper   Glue   Scissors   Pencil

1

2

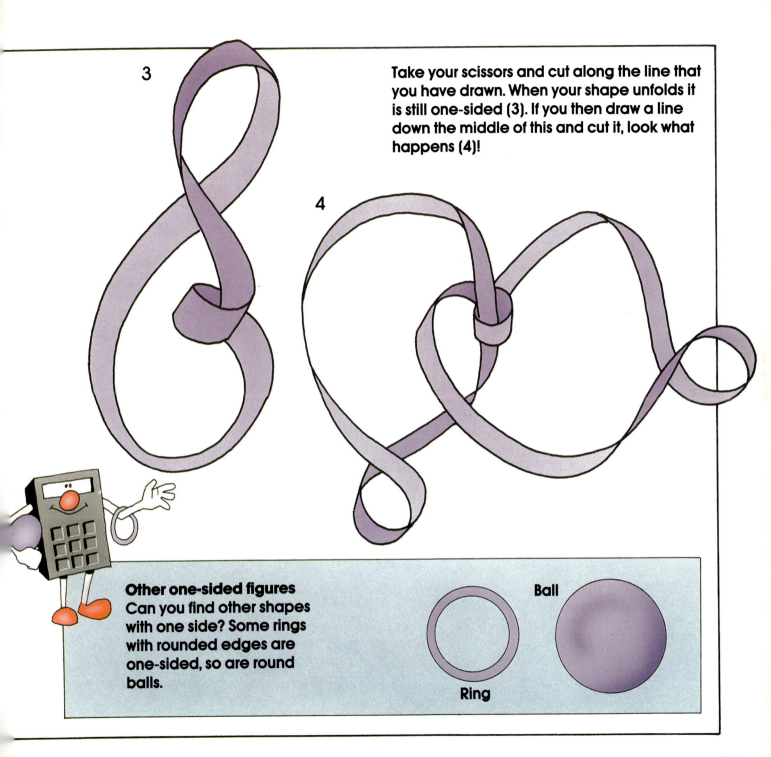

3

Take your scissors and cut along the line that you have drawn. When your shape unfolds it is still one-sided (3). If you then draw a line down the middle of this and cut it, look what happens (4)!

4

Other one-sided figures
Can you find other shapes with one side? Some rings with rounded edges are one-sided, so are round balls.

Ball

Ring

MAKING A CUBE

A "net" is a shape which can be cut out, folded and stuck together to make a solid shape. Here is a way you can use one to make a cube.

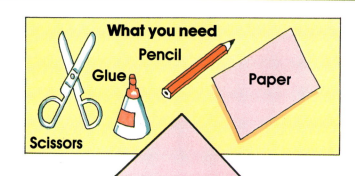

What you need

Scissors

Glue

Pencil

Paper

What to do
Trace this net on to thin card or paper. Cut around it and fold along the dotted lines. Bend the flaps over carefully. Now you are ready to glue.

To trace this, see pg. 13.

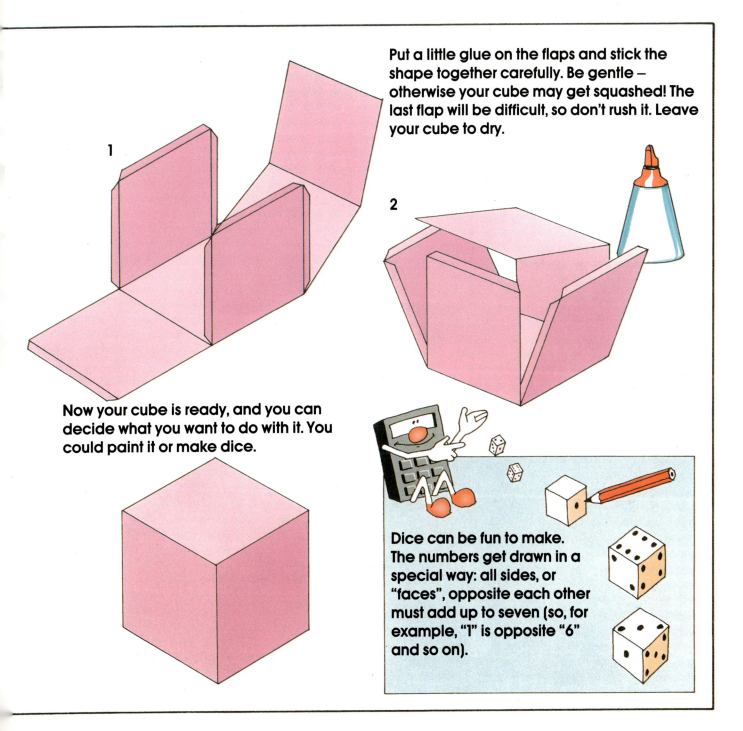

1

Put a little glue on the flaps and stick the shape together carefully. Be gentle – otherwise your cube may get squashed! The last flap will be difficult, so don't rush it. Leave your cube to dry.

2

Now your cube is ready, and you can decide what you want to do with it. You could paint it or make dice.

Dice can be fun to make. The numbers get drawn in a special way: all sides, or "faces", opposite each other must add up to seven (so, for example, "1" is opposite "6" and so on).

OTHER SOLID SHAPES

Many solids can be made from card "nets" (see pg. 26) and then turned into things like calendars, decorations and so on. Here are some ideas for you to try.

What to do
Trace "A" and "B" on to thin card. Cut them out and fold along the dotted lines.

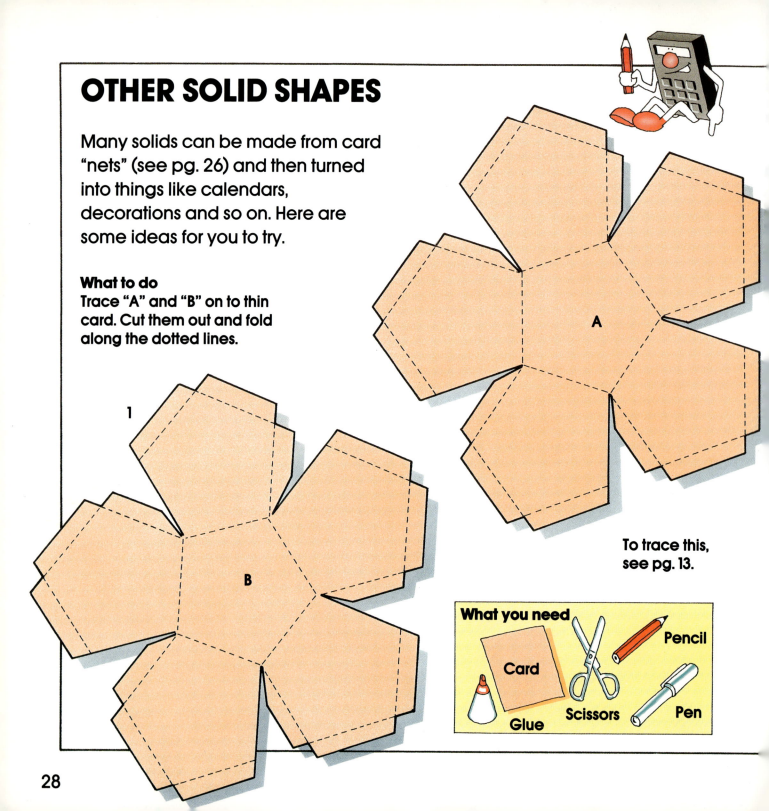

1

B

A

To trace this, see pg. 13.

What you need

Card

Glue

Scissors

Pencil

Pen

2

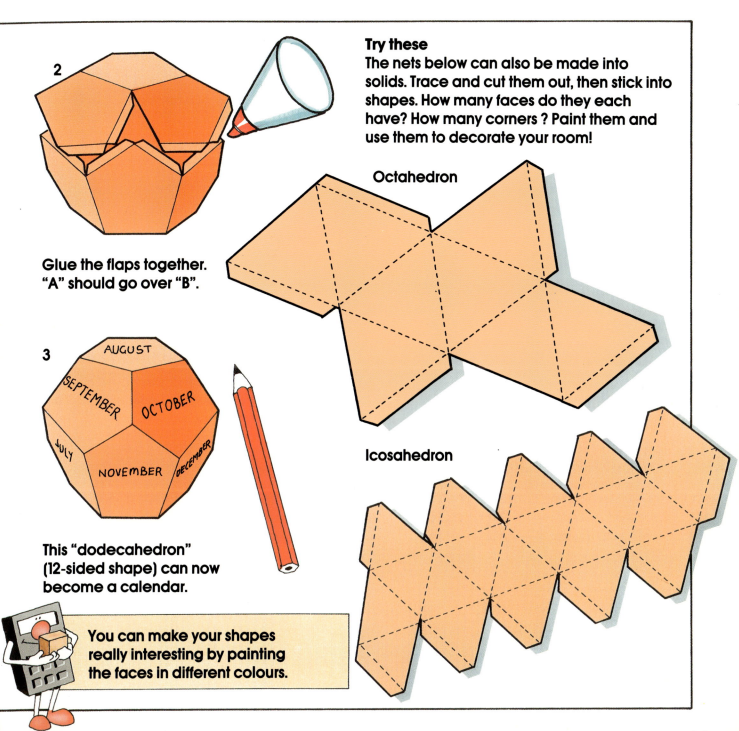

Glue the flaps together.
"A" should go over "B".

3

This "dodecahedron"
(12-sided shape) can now
become a calendar.

AUGUST
SEPTEMBER
OCTOBER
JULY
NOVEMBER
DECEMBER

You can make your shapes
really interesting by painting
the faces in different colours.

Try these
The nets below can also be made into
solids. Trace and cut them out, then stick into
shapes. How many faces do they each
have? How many corners ? Paint them and
use them to decorate your room!

Octahedron

Icosahedron

SHAPES AND SOLIDS

Some shapes are flat (2-dimensional). Many get their names from the number of sides they have. For example, an octogon has eight sides.

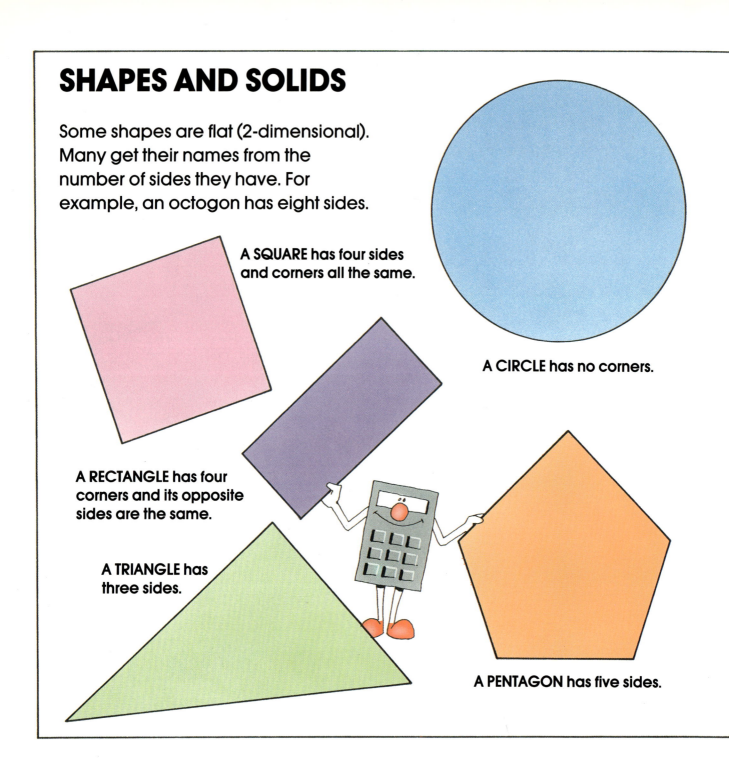

A SQUARE has four sides and corners all the same.

A CIRCLE has no corners.

A RECTANGLE has four corners and its opposite sides are the same.

A TRIANGLE has three sides.

A PENTAGON has five sides.

Solids are 3-dimensional. Sometimes they are named by the number of faces they have.

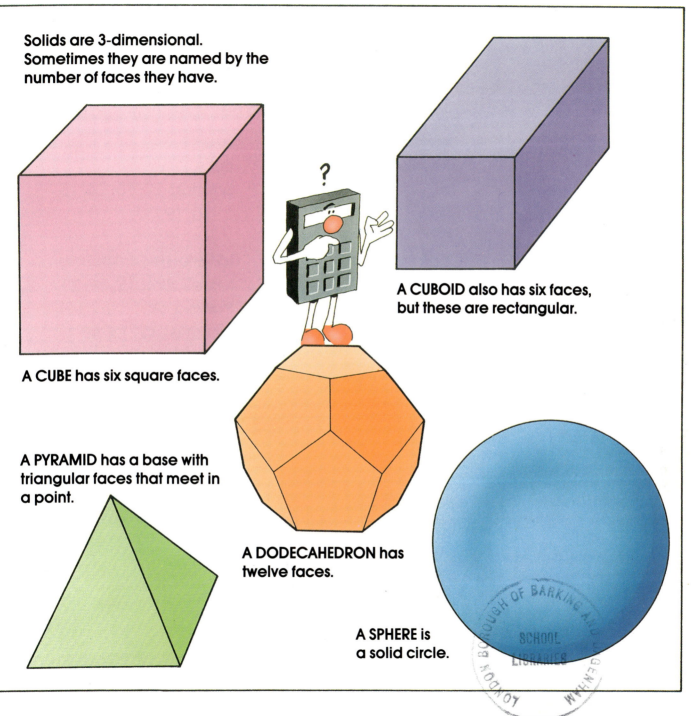

A CUBE has six square faces.

A CUBOID also has six faces, but these are rectangular.

A PYRAMID has a base with triangular faces that meet in a point.

A DODECAHEDRON has twelve faces.

A SPHERE is a solid circle.

31

INDEX

ANSWERS

Page 13: Which shapes? Rectangle, square, parallelogram, triangle.

The two smallest triangles are exactly the same.

There are two rectangles, two parallelograms and four triangles that are the same shape but different sizes.

Page 17: The first and second shapes are the same size – they both have an area of 20 sq. cm.

The largest shape in group A is the green square. The largest shape in group B is the blue trapezium.

Page 29: The octahedron has 8 faces.
The icosahedron has 20 faces.

Page 29

PRINTED IN BELGIUM BY
proost
INTERNATIONAL BOOK PRODUCTION